everyday
tofu

from
pancakes
to
pizza

Gary Landgrebe

THE CROSSING PRESS
FREEDOM, CALIFORNIA

©2000 Gary Landgrebe
Cover photograph ©1999 Thompson + Narita
Cover designed by Victoria May
Interior designed by Courtnay Perry
Interior photographs ©1999 Thompson + Narita on pp. 5, 13, 18, 41, 47, 61, 62, 65, 79, 81, 86.
Interior photographs ©1999 Digital Stock on pp. 23, 42, 45, 57, 59, 68, 83, 91, 94, 106.
Interior photographs ©1999 PhotoDisc on pp. 21, 26, 31, 35, 38, 50, 53, 67, 73, 76, 93, 99, 102.
Printed in the USA

For information on bulk purchases or group discounts for this and other Crossing Press titles, please contact our Special Sales Manager at 800/777-1048.

Visit our web site at: **www.crossingpress.com**

Library of Congress Cataloging-in-Publication Data

Landgrebe, Gary
    Everyday tofu: from pancakes to pizza / by Gary Landgrebe.
        p. cm.
    Includes index.
    ISBN 1-58091-047-5 (pbk.)
    1. Cookery (Tofu). I. Title.
TX814.5.T63L38   1999
641.6'5655--dc21   99-33921
                                     CIP

This book is dedicated

to the one in all

who waits so patiently

for all to be at one

with all that is

A special thanks goes out to Seraphina for much love and light along with all her help; to Junauro and Oradona for patience and a willingness to change; and to Anna, Connie, Christmas, Gene, Marie, and Theresa for the energy and love they gave.

Contents

When I started to use tofu, I tried two or three recipes a day. It was always rewarding to have people rave about the results. Today I am ever more impressed with the versatility and adaptability of tofu. It offers so many possibilities that I cannot help being thankful for having had the chance to work so closely with it.

Gary Landgrebe

Foreword

I remember the first time I saw tofu in the vegetable section at the market. The produce man told me it was made from soybeans, had almost no flavor, and was used in Oriental dishes. He said he stocked it in the produce section because it was often used with vegetables and needed to be refrigerated.

Intrigued by this strange, water-bathed food, I arranged to visit a tofu factory where I could actually see tofu being made. The process looked quite simple—similar to cheese making. The family making the tofu was very enthusiastic. They called tofu "meat without the bone," and told me that people in the Orient had been eating it for centuries as one of their main protein staples.

The more I found out about tofu, the more impressed I became. It is low in calories, high in good-quality protein, and rich in both calcium and iron. I introduced it to my family in a few salad dressings, soups, and dinner loaves—no objections, but no raves either. I was getting frustrated because I couldn't find many ways to use tofu in my everyday cooking.

I began to try Gary Landgrebe's recipes and was sold right away! My family was a bit wary at first—"This couldn't have tofu in it, it tastes so good,"...or "Whoever heard of tofu in bread. Can I have another piece?"

Gary has chosen a food just right for our times—low in calories, high in nutrients, inexpensive, and ecologically positive in all respects. He has combined it with well-known, widely enjoyed ingredients to create tasty, American-style dishes. His recipes are easy to follow and offer great variety: delicate (Mushroom Crepes) to spicy (Chili Con Tofu), crispy (Tofu Croutons) to silky smooth (Tofu Custard). Even the hard-to-please eater will find delights in this book.

Tofu

Soybeans are soaked for several hours and then puréed with water. The purée is brought to a boil in a large pot and then strained through a cloth. The crude fibers of the soybean are caught in the cloth and discarded. The remaining liquid, called soy milk, is returned to the pot. After it has simmered for a few minutes a small amount of solidifier is added. This causes the milk to separate into curds and whey. The curds are ladled into molds, pressed into the familiar shape and chilled. Through this simple process the highly nutritious essence of the soybean becomes available to our bodies in a form that can be easily utilized.

The tofu called for in this book is the fresh, creamy white kind. There are two basic types of tofu: the softer Chinese (set with calcium sulfate, the purified form of gypsum) and the harder Japanese (set with nigari, the natural by-product of salt making). Either of these may be used successfully in these recipes.

Buying Tofu

The flavor and texture of tofu are determined by its freshness and the type of solidifier used. When buying tofu, check the date on the package; it usually indicates the date before which the tofu should be used. Ask your grocer to be sure. The fresher the tofu, the sweeter and lighter its flavor. As tofu ages it develops a distinctive tang. This may add character to a main dish, but for breads and desserts use only the freshest tofu.

Storing Tofu

Tofu must be covered with water and refrigerated to stay fresh. It can be kept unopened in its original package for 7–10 days. Once opened, however, the tofu should be transferred to another covered container, rinsed well, and covered with fresh water. The water should be changed daily.

Frozen Tofu

If you have more tofu on hand than you can use within the recommended time, freeze it!

Tofu may be frozen in its original container just as it comes from the store. After it has been in the freezer for a week, its texture changes from soft and custard-like to spongy. In this state it can be crumbled or sliced and used as a substitute for ground meats or pasta.

Before frozen tofu is used, it should be thoroughly thawed (but not left indefinitely at room temperature), drained of all liquid, rinsed, and squeezed dry. When frozen tofu is called for here, it is listed in terms of its weight before freezing.

Tofu as a Protein Source

Four ounces of fresh tofu contain 8.8 grams of high-quality protein, comparable to chicken or steak in its usefulness to the body. Tofu's protein potential can be further enhanced if it is served with milk, eggs, cheese, grains (such as millet or wheat, especially wheat bran, oats, and rice), cornmeal, sesame or sunflower seeds, or vegetables such as spinach and corn. All the recipes in here illustrate how easy it is to combine these foods with tofu to achieve a protein usability higher than that found in most other foods.

Tofu as a Diet Food

Tofu is an ideal food for weight watchers. An eight-ounce serving contains only 147–164 calories, but provides over one-fourth of the suggested daily protein allowance for an adult male, as well as an abundance of other vitamins and minerals.

Tofu and Digestibility

Since tofu is made from soybeans you might wonder about its digestibility. You'll be happy to know that the hard to digest crude fibers and water-soluble carbohydrates found in soybeans are automatically removed during the tofu-making process. Tofu is an excellent food for babies, surgical recuperees, and other people with special digestive needs.

A Nutritional Profile

8 ounces of tofu provide the same amount of usable protein as
> 3¼ oz. steak
> 5½ oz. hamburger
> 1⅔ cup milk
> 2 eggs
> 2 oz. cheese

8 ounces of tofu provide about the same amount of calcium as
> 8 oz. of milk—Great for people who don't like or can't drink milk!

8 ounces of tofu provide about the same amount of iron as
> 4½ eggs
> 2 oz. beef liver

Sharon Elliot

tofumain dishes

spaghetti
sauce

Sauté for about 5 minutes in 2 tbs. olive oil

    1 large onion

    4 large cloves garlic, minced

Add   1 lb. soft tofu, mashed well with a fork

    1 can (15 oz.) tomato sauce

    1 can (28 oz.) tomatoes

    1 bay leaf

    1½ tsp. Italian seasoning or ½ tsp. each oregano, basil, and thyme

    ¼ tsp. pepper

    1 tbs. beef-flavored bouillon

    ½–1 cup sliced mushrooms

Bring to a boil, reduce heat and simmer, covered, for 30 minutes. Stir frequently.

asian delight

SERVES 4–5

Good with steamed millet* or rice.

Sauté for about 3 minutes in 3 tbs. peanut or light-colored sesame oil

>   1 large onion, thinly sliced
>   2 cloves garlic, minced

Add   1 cup water

>   3 tbs. soy sauce
>   1 tbs. beef-flavored bouillon
>   1 tbs. + 1 tsp. light molasses
>   2 tbs. peanut butter
>   ¼ tsp. cardamom
>   ⅛ tsp. nutmeg
>   ¼ cup raisins
>   ¼ cup cashew pieces, lightly toasted

Stir until the peanut butter is well blended.

Add   1 lb. firm tofu, diced in ¼-inch cubes

>   2 medium bananas, sliced in half lengthwise
>   and then in ½-inch pieces

Simmer for 5 minutes, stirring frequently.

---

* Millet complements the protein in tofu extremely well. It is similar to rice in flavor, but millet has more protein and iron and fewer calories. Millet is not readily available in all supermarkets, but it can be found in natural food stores and health food stores as well as in Oriental specialty shops. To prepare millet, use 3–3 ½ times as much water as grain. Cook, covered, for about 30 minutes. For a nutty-flavored millet, sauté in a bit of oil before adding the water and cooking.

tofu
cheese sauce

Mix in a blender until smooth

    ½ cup milk

    12 oz. soft tofu

    ½ tsp. salt

    ½ tsp. dry mustard

    ¼ tsp. paprika

    Freshly ground pepper or a little cayenne

Melt in a large saucepan

    1 tbs. butter

Pour the tofu mixture into the pan.

Add   1½ cups grated cheddar cheese

    1 tbs. grated Parmesan cheese

Stir until the cheese has melted and the mixture is bubbly.

tofu rarebit

Mix in a blender until smooth

    1 can (15 oz.) tomato sauce

    1 lb. soft tofu

    1 tsp. dry mustard

    1 tsp. Worcestershire sauce

    ½ tsp. salt

    ¼ tsp. paprika

    Freshly ground pepper or cayenne

Warm in a heavy skillet over medium heat

    1 tbs. oil

Pour the tofu mixture into the skillet.

Add   2–3 cups grated aged cheese

Stir until the cheese has melted and the mixture is bubbly. Ladle over toast or crackers.

cannelloni

Cook and drain

    8 manicotti shells

Mix well in a large bowl

    1 lb. soft tofu, mashed well with a fork

    1 egg, lightly beaten

    1½ tsp. dried parsley

    ½ tsp. nutmeg

    ½ tsp. dried basil

    ½ tsp. salt

    ¼ tsp. pepper

    ¼ cup grated Parmesan cheese

    1 cup grated cheddar cheese

Fill the manicotti shells with the tofu mixture.

Lay the manicotti down the center of an oiled 9-inch x 13-inch baking dish.

Cover with

    1 can (15 oz.) Italian-style tomato sauce

        (mixed with any remaining stuffing).

Sprinkle with

    Grated Parmesan cheese

Bake at 350° for 30 minutes.

mushroom
skillet bake

Sauté in 2–3 tbs. oil in a large oven-proof skillet
over medium heat

    1 medium onion, chopped

Add and sauté for 3 minutes more

    4 cups sliced mushrooms (tightly packed)

Remove from heat.

Stir in   12 oz. soft tofu, mashed well with a fork

    ½ cup milk

    3 eggs, lightly beaten

    1 tsp. salt

    ¼ tsp. pepper

    ¼ tsp. garlic powder

    1 cup grated cheese or Swiss cheese

Bake at 350° for 30–35 minutes.

mexican
cheese pie

SERVES 6–8

THE CRUST
(OPTIONAL)

Prepare your favorite single, 10-inch crust.

Prick well with a fork.

Bake at 450° for 7 minutes.

THE FILLING

Mix in a blender until smooth

1½ lbs. soft tofu

1 cup buttermilk

1 can (6 oz.) tomato paste

1 tbs. honey

2 eggs

1¼ tsp. salt

½–¾ tsp. cumin (to taste)

¼ tsp. paprika

¼ tsp. coriander

¼ tsp. cayenne

2 tbs. flour

Pour into a large bowl.

Stir in   2 tbs. dehydrated onion flakes

1½ cups grated cheddar cheese

¼ cup grated Parmesan cheese

2 cups grated Monterey Jack cheese

1 can (4½ oz.) chopped black olives, drained

Turn into the prepared crust or a 10-inch baking dish.

Bake at 325° for 1 hour.

Let stand for 15 minutes before serving.

tofu **chili cheese**squares

Mix in a blender until smooth

> 3 eggs
>
> ¾ lbs. soft tofu
>
> ¾ tsp. salt

Turn into a large bowl.

Stir in   1 lb. cheddar cheese, grated

> 1 can (4 oz.) chopped green chilis, drained

Spread evenly in an oiled 9-inch x 13-inch pan.

Sprinkle with

> Grated Parmesan cheese

Dust with

> Paprika

Bake at 350° for 30–35 minutes.

italian
nonmeat balls

These are real proof that it doesn't have to be meat to be Italian!

Mix well in a large bowl

> 1 lb. soft tofu, mashed well with a fork
>
> 2 eggs, lightly beaten
>
> ½ cup fine fresh bread crumbs
>
> 2 tsp. beef-flavored bouillon
>
> ½ tsp. onion salt
>
> ½ tsp. Italian seasoning or ¼ tsp. each dried oregano and basil
>
> ½ tsp. garlic powder
>
> 3 tbs. grated Parmesan cheese
>
> 1 tbs. dehydrated onion flakes
>
> ¼ tsp. pepper
>
> ⅛ tsp. nutmeg

Form into 1-inch balls.

Brown the balls in oil.

Use with your favorite spaghetti recipe or place the balls in an oiled baking dish and cover them halfway with your favorite Italian-style tomato sauce.

Bake at 350° for 30 minutes.

spinach pie

**THE CRUST
(OPTIONAL)**

Prepare your favorite unsweetened, double, 10-inch crust (optional).

THE FILLING

Thaw
      10–12 oz. frozen chopped spinach
Drain and squeeze well.
Add   1 lb. soft tofu, mashed well with the fork
       2 eggs, lightly beaten
       2½ cups grated cheddar cheese
       1½ tsp. salt
Turn into the prepared crust or a 10-inch oiled casserole. If a crust is used, top with the upper crust, flute the edges and prick with a fork.
Bake at 450° for 10 minutes, reduce heat to 350° and bake an additional 45–50 minutes.
If a crust is not used, bake at 350° for 30–40 minutes.

italian
cheese pie

THE CRUST
(OPTIONAL)

Prepare your favorite single 9-inch crust. Bake at 425° for 10 minutes.

THE FILLING

Mix in a blender until smooth

2 eggs

1 lb. soft tofu

¾ tsp. salt

¾ tsp. Italian seasoning or ¼ tsp. each dried oregano, basil, and thyme

¼ tsp. garlic powder

1 can (8 oz.) tomato sauce

Turn the tofu mixture into a large bowl.

Stir in ½ cup grated Parmesan cheese

½ cup grated mozzarella cheese

Spread evenly in the prepared crust or in a 9-inch casserole.

Top with 6–8 oz. mozzarella cheese, thinly sliced

Bake at 350° for 30–40 minutes or until set and browned.

baked italian
eggplant skillet

Sauté in 2 tbs. oil, in a large oven-proof skillet over medium heat

> 1 medium onion, chopped
>
> 4 cloves garlic, minced

Add 1 eggplant, diced in ¼-inch cubes

> 1 can (8 oz.) tomato sauce
>
> ¼ cup water
>
> 2 tsp. chicken-flavored bouillon
>
> ¾ tsp. Italian seasoning or ¼ tsp. each dried oregano, basil, and thyme
>
> ¼ tsp. garlic powder

Bring to a boil, reduce heat, and simmer, covered, for 10 minutes. While the eggplant is simmering, mix together in a large bowl

> 1 lb. soft tofu, mashed well with a fork
>
> 3 eggs, lightly beaten
>
> 1 cup grated cheese

When the eggplant has simmered for 10 minutes, stir in the tofu mixture.

Sprinkle with

> Grated Parmesan cheese

Bake at 350° for 35 minutes.

tofu
tamale pie

Sauté in 3 tbs. oil, in a 5-quart pan

> 1 onion, chopped
>
> 1 medium bell pepper, chopped
>
> 3 large cloves garlic, minced

Remove from heat.

Stir in 2 lbs. soft tofu, mashed well with a fork

> 2 cans (16 oz. each) tomatoes, broken up
>
> 1 can (4½ oz.) chopped black olives
>
> 2 cups corn kernels
>
> ¾ cup water
>
> 2 tbs. chili powder
>
> 2 tbs. beef-flavored bouillon
>
> ¾ tsp. salt
>
> ¾ tsp. garlic powder
>
> ½ tsp. cumin
>
> ¼ tsp. pepper
>
> 1 cup cornmeal

Bake at 350° for 45 minutes.

Remove from oven.

Top with 8 oz. Monterey Jack cheese, thinly sliced

Return to the oven for an additional 15 minutes.

weight watcher's
mexican-style lunch

SERVES 4

Soak in a medium-sized, stainless steel or glass bowl
for 30 minutes

> 1 cup chopped onion
> ½ cup apple cider vinegar

Drain well.

Mix in a blender until smooth

> 1 lb. soft tofu
> 2 cups tomato sauce
> 1 tsp. salt
> 1 tsp. cumin
> ⅛ tsp. cloves
> 2 cloves garlic

Turn the tofu mixture into a large bowl.

Stir in   the drained onion

> 1 cup finely chopped bell pepper
> 1 cup grated cheddar cheese

Spread evenly in a 2-quart casserole.

Bake at 350° for 1 hour.

creamed
corn custard

Mix in a blender until smooth

    1 lb. soft tofu

    3–4 eggs

    2 tbs. butter

    2 tbs. honey

    ½ tsp. salt

    ¼–½ tsp. pepper

    ¼ cup whole wheat flour

    ¼ cup instant nonfat milk powder

Add   2 cups whole kernel corn, cooked and

        drained (save the liquor)

    ¾ cup corn liquor (or water)

Blend again until the mixture resembles a fine grade of creamed corn.

Turn into an oiled 10-inch baking dish.

Bake at 350° for 50–60 minutes.

tofu nut loaf
or stuffing

Sauté in 4–6 tbs. butter* for about 5 minutes

    1 onion, chopped

    1½ cups chopped celery

    3 cloves garlic, minced

Remove from heat.

Add   1 lb. soft tofu, mashed well with a fork

    2 cups cooked millet** or rice

    1 cup chopped walnuts

    1 cup chopped cashews

    ¼ cup sesame seeds, toasted

    1 tsp. dried parsley

    ¼ tsp. dried rosemary

    ½ tsp. dried sage

    1½ tsp. salt

    ½ tsp. pepper

    3 eggs, lightly beaten

Turn into an oiled 9-inch by 5-inch loaf pan.

Bake at 350° for about 40 minutes.

---

*If using as a stuffing, you may wish to add another 4 tbs. butter.

**See page 15.

tofu **casserole**
al italiano

Mix in a blender until smooth

    1 lb. soft tofu

    3 eggs

    1 can (8 oz.) tomato sauce

    2–4 cloves garlic

    2 tsp. dried basil

    1 tsp. salt

    ¼ tsp. nutmeg

    2 tbs. onion powder

    ¼ tsp. pepper

    2–4 tbs. grated Parmesan cheese

Add and blend again

    2 tbs. flour

Add   1 bell pepper, finely chopped

    1 cup chopped green onion

Mix in well with a long-handled spoon.

Turn half the tofu mixture into an oiled 2-quart casserole.

Cover with half the slices from

    8 oz. Mozzarella cheese, thinly sliced

Spread the remaining tofu mixture over the cheese slices. Top with the remaining cheese.

Bake at 350° for 50–60 minutes or until golden brown.

potato bake
with cheese

SERVES 4

Mix gently in a large bowl

    ½ cup chopped green onion

    2 cups cooked potatoes, sliced or diced

    1 lb. soft tofu, mashed well with a fork

    2 eggs, lightly beaten

    1 cup sour cream

    1 cup grated cheddar cheese

    2 tsp. seasoned or herb salt

Turn into an oiled 2-quart casserole.

Bake at 350° for 50–60 minutes.

tofu quiche

**THE CRUST
(OPTIONAL)**

Mix together in a medium bowl

35 Saltine crackers, crushed

¼–½ cup melted butter

Press into a 9-inch spring form pan.

Chill until needed.

THE FILLING

Mix in a blender until smooth

½ cup milk

3 eggs

1½ lbs. soft tofu

3 tbs. flour

2 tbs. onion powder

1 tsp. salt

1 tsp. Worcestershire sauce

¼ tsp. pepper or cayenne

Add and mix in well with a long-handled spoon

2 cups grated Swiss cheese

Turn into the prepared crust or a 9-inch oiled casserole.

Bake at 350° for 1 hour.

onion torte

THE CRUST
(OPTIONAL)

Mix together in a medium bowl
      35 Saltine crackers, crushed
      ¼–½ cup melted butter
Press into an 8-inch or 9-inch spring form pan.
Chill until needed.

THE FILLING

Sauté in 2–3 tbs. butter until golden
      5 medium onions, sliced
Spread the onions evenly on the bottom of the crust or
in the bottom of an oiled 9-inch baking dish.
Mix in a blender until smooth
      4 eggs
      1 lb. soft tofu
      1¼ tsp. salt
      1 tsp. dried parsley
      ¼ tsp. pepper or cayenne
      ¼ tsp. bitters (optional)
Pour into a large bowl.
Stir in   2–3 cups grated cheddar cheese
Spread gently over the onions.
Dust with
      Paprika
Bake at 350° for 50–60 minutes.

green olive
chili casserole

Good hot or cold!

Layer half of each of the following ingredients, in order, in an oiled 9-inch x 13-inch baking dish

> 1 bag (7 oz.) natural corn chips
>
> 2 cups grated Monterey Jack cheese
>
> 2 cups grated cheddar cheese
>
> 2 cans (4 oz. each) chopped green chilis, drained
>
> 1 can (15 oz). green olives (pitted or stuffed), drained and sliced

Repeat the layers.

Mix either of the following combinations in a blender until smooth

FILLING VARIATION #1:

> 6 eggs
>
> 2 cups milk
>
> 1 lb. tofu
>
> 1 tsp. dry mustard
>
> 1 tsp. salt

Filling variation #2 with tomato sauce and spice:

> 1 can (16 oz.) tomato sauce
>
> 1 lb. soft tofu
>
> 6 eggs
>
> 2 tsp. cumin
>
> 1½ tsp. onion salt
>
> ½ tsp. dried oregano
>
> ¼ tsp. pepper

Pour the mixture evenly over the layers.

Refrigerate for at least 4 hours. May be refrigerated overnight.

Bake at 350° for 1 hour.

spicy
skillet bake

Sauté in 2 tbs. oil, in a large oven-proof skillet over medium heat

> 1 large onion, finely chopped
>
> 1 large bell pepper, finely chopped

Remove from heat.

Stir in   1 lb. soft tofu, mashed well with a fork

> 1 can (8 oz.) tomato sauce
>
> 4 eggs, lightly beaten
>
> 1½ tsp. cumin
>
> 2 tsp. chili powder
>
> 1 tsp. salt
>
> ½ tsp. garlic powder
>
> 1 cup grated cheddar cheese

Bake at 375° for 45 minutes.

tofu pan pizza

Mix in a blender until smooth

    1 lb. soft tofu

    2 eggs

    1 tbs. oil

    ½ tsp. salt

Add and mix again

    1½ cups whole wheat flour

    2 tsp. baking powder

Spread the dough out on a 12-inch oiled pizza pan or baking sheet.

Spoon on Special Sauce (see below).

SPECIAL SAUCE

Sauté in 3 tbs. oil

    1 cup chopped onion

    1 cup chopped bell pepper

    2 cloves garlic, minced

Add   1 can (15 oz.) tomato sauce

    ½ tsp. salt

    1 tsp. dried Italian seasoning or ½ tsp. each dried oregano and basil

Bring to a boil, reduce heat, and simmer 20–30 minutes —until very thick.

tofu dip

Mix in a blender until smooth

> 8 oz. soft tofu
>
> 1 cup sour cream
>
> 1 tbs. onion salt
>
> 1 tbs. dehydrated onion flakes
>
> 1½ tsp. garlic powder
>
> 2 tbs. grated Parmesan cheese

Add and mix in well with a long-handled spoon, for texture

> 1 tbs. dehydrated onion flakes

Refrigerate for several hours before serving.

tofu hummus

This is an adaptation of a dish from the Mideast which is delicious eaten on its own, served as a dip for raw veggies, or used as a spread for bread or crackers. If you are not already familiar with tahini (similar to peanut butter, but made from sesame seeds), this recipe will provide you with an opportunity to become so. It is available in some supermarkets, but is most often found in delicatessens and health food stores. Sesame seeds are an ideal protein complement for tofu.

Mix in a blender until smooth. Use a spatula to keep the mixture in the blades if necessary.

- 1 lb. soft tofu
- 1 cup tahini
- ¾ cup lemon juice
- 2 tsp. salt
- 2 cloves garlic

Refrigerate for several hours before serving.

Serve garnished with

- Chopped fresh parsley

frozen tofu main dishes

huevos
rancheros

Sauté for about 5 minutes in 2 tbs. oil (olive, preferably)

    1 onion, chopped

    1 bell pepper, chopped

    3–4 cloves garlic, minced

Add   1 can (15 oz.) tomato sauce

    ½ cup water

    1 lb. frozen firm tofu, thawed, rinsed,

       squeezed dry, and crumbled

    ½ tsp. dried oregano

    ½ tsp. chili powder

    ½ tsp. cumin

    2 tsp. beef-flavored bouillon

    ¼ tsp. pepper

Bring to a boil, reduce heat, and simmer, covered, for 10 minutes.

Make four indentations in the thick tofu sauce; break an egg into each one.

Simmer, covered, 5–10 minutes more—until the eggs are poached as desired.

Spoon into 4 bowls.

meal
in a skillet

Sauté for about 5 minutes in 1–2 tbs. olive oil

    1 medium onion, chopped

    ½ medium bell pepper, chopped

    2–4 cloves garlic, minced

Add   1 can (28 oz.) tomatoes, broken up

    1 bay leaf

    ½ tsp. dried basil

    ½ tsp. dried oregano

    ½ tsp. salt

    ¼ tsp. pepper

    ½–1 cup sliced mushrooms

    1½ lbs. frozen firm tofu, thawed, rinsed,
        squeezed dry, and crumbled

Bring to a boil, reduce heat, and simmer, covered, for 30 minutes.

Remove from heat and add slowly, stirring constantly

    2–4 eggs, lightly beaten

Continue stirring until the entrée is smooth and thickened.

baked
chili relleno

SERVES 4–6

Sauté in 1 tbs. oil

> 1 onion, chopped

Remove from heat and stir in

> 1½ lbs. frozen firm tofu, thawed, rinsed,
> squeezed dry, and crumbled
>
> 1 tsp. beef-flavored bouillon
>
> ¼ tsp. salt
>
> ¼ tsp. pepper

Mix well in a medium-sized bowl

> 4 eggs, lightly beaten
>
> 1½ cups milk
>
> ¼ cup whole wheat flour
>
> ¼ tsp. salt
>
> ¼ tsp. pepper

Layer half of each of the following, in order, in an oiled
8-inch x 8-inch baking dish

> 2 cans (4 oz. each) chopped green chilis,
> drained
>
> 2 cups grated cheddar cheese
>
> The tofu mixture

Repeat the layers.

Pour the egg mixture evenly over the casserole.

Bake at 350° for 50–60 minutes or until a toothpick
inserted in the center comes out clean.

chili con tofu

Sauté in 2–3 tbs. oil

    1 medium onion, chopped

    2 cloves garlic, minced

Add   2 cans (16 oz. each) tomatoes, broken up

    3½ cups cooked kidney beans*

    1¼ cups bean liquor (or water)*

    2 tsp. beef-flavored bouillon

    2 tsp. chili powder (or more, to taste)

    ½ tsp. cumin

    ¾ tsp. salt (or about 1¼ tsp. if the beans used
        have not been salted)

    1 bay leaf

    1 tsp. honey

    2 lbs. frozen firm tofu, thawed, rinsed,
        squeezed dry, and crumbled

Bring to a boil, reduce heat, and simmer, covered,
for 1 hour.

---

* 2 cans (16 oz. each) kidney beans, undrained, can be substituted
for cooked beans and bean liquor.

enchiladas

Best baked a day ahead and reheated.

THE SAUCE

Sauté in 1–3 tbs. olive oil
    1 large onion, chopped
    2 medium bell peppers, chopped
    4 cloves garlic, minced

Add 3 cans (8 oz. each) tomato sauce
    3 bay leaves
    2 tsp. beef-flavored bouillon
    1 tsp.–1 tbs. cumin powder (to taste)
    ¼ tsp. ground cloves
    ¼ tsp. salt

Bring to a boil, reduce heat and simmer, covered, for 30 minutes.

THE FILLING

Soak in a large stainless steel or glass bowl for 30 minutes 2 small onions, chopped
    ½ cup apple cider or wine vinegar

Drain well.

Stir in 2 lbs. frozen firm tofu, thawed, rinsed, squeezed dry, and crumbled
    2 cans (4½ oz. each) chopped black olives
    1 tsp. salt
    1 tsp. garlic powder
    2 cups grated sharp cheddar cheese

THE GARNISHES

1½ cups shredded iceberg lettuce

2 cups grated sharp cheddar cheese

8 hard boiled eggs, sliced in rounds

ASSEMBLING THE ENCHILADAS

12 flour tortillas

Heat a tortilla in an ungreased skillet over medium-hot heat until soft (a few seconds on each side).

Dip the heated tortilla into the prepared sauce.

Fill each tortilla with

½ cup filling

Garnish with

2 tbs. shredded lettuce

1–2 tbs. grated cheddar cheese

6–7 egg rounds

Roll the tortilla around the filling.

When all the tortillas have been filled, place them close together, seam-side down, in a large baking dish.

Cover with the remaining prepared sauce.

Top with the remaining garnish cheese plus

2 cups grated Monterey Jack cheese

Bake, covered, at 350° for 1 hour.

Refrigerate overnight.

Reheat, covered, at 350° for 30–35 minutes.

stuffed
bell peppers

Sauté for about 5 minutes in 1–2 tbs. olive oil

    1 large onion, chopped

    2 cloves garlic, minced

Remove from heat and stir in

    1 lb. frozen firm tofu, thawed, rinsed,
        squeezed dry, and crumbled

    1 can (15 oz.) tomato sauce

    ½ tsp. salt

    ¼ tsp. dried basil

    ¼ tsp. dried sage

    ¼ tsp. pepper

    ½ cup grated sharp cheese

When slightly cooled add slowly, stirring constantly

    3 eggs, lightly beaten

Spoon the mixture into

    4 large bell peppers, stemmed and seeded

Place the peppers upright in a baking dish and pour in

    ¾ cup boiling water

Bake at 350° for 1 hour or until the peppers are tender when pierced with a fork.

(Add more water during baking if necessary.)

tofu a la king

Good over hot millet.*

Sauté in 2 tbs. butter or oil, in a large skillet over medium heat

    1 medium onion, chopped

    ¼ cup chopped green pepper

    3 cups thinly sliced mushrooms

Mix in a blender until smooth

    3 cups milk

    8 oz. cream cheese, at room temperature

    2–3 tbs. dry sherry

    1 cup instant nonfat milk powder

    3 tbs. arrowroot or cornstarch

    1 tbs. + 1 tsp. chicken-flavored bouillon

    ¼ tsp. salt

    ¼ tsp. pepper

Pour the blended ingredients into the skillet.

Add 2 lbs. frozen firm tofu, thawed, rinsed, squeezed dry, and crumbled

Mix well.

Bring to a boil and simmer, stirring constantly, until thickened (about 2 minutes).

---

* See page 15.

potato cheese
chowder

SERVES 4–6

Sauté in 1–3 tbs. oil for 3 minutes
    1 medium onion, chopped
    2–4 cloves garlic, minced
Add and sauté for an additional 2 minutes
    3 medium potatoes, diced in ½-inch cubes
Add   2 cans (8 oz. each) tomato sauce
    4 cups water
    1 lb. frozen firm tofu, thawed, rinsed,
        squeezed dry, and crumbled
    ¼ tsp. salt
    1 tsp. beef-flavored bouillon
Bring to a boil, reduce heat and simmer, covered, for 20 minutes or until the potatoes are cooked but not mushy.
Remove from heat and stir in
    1¼ cups grated cheddar cheese
Stir until the cheese is melted and well integrated with the other ingredients.

cheesy
zucchini puff

Steam until tender

    3 medium zucchini, cut in slices or chunks

Mix together in a large bowl

    1 cup (4 oz.) grated cheddar cheese

    12 oz. frozen firm tofu, thawed, rinsed,
        squeezed dry, and crumbled

    2 eggs, lightly beaten

    ¾ tsp. salt

    ¾ tsp. dried dill weed

    ½ cup croutons

Add and stir gently

    The zucchini, well drained

Turn into a shallow, oiled 1½-quart casserole.

Bake at 350° for 30 minutes.

noodleless
lasagna

THE SAUCE

Sauté in ¼ cup olive oil

    4 onions, chopped

    4 cloves garlic, minced

Add   2 cans (15 oz. each) tomato sauce

    1 can (16 oz.) tomatoes, broken up

    2 tsp. beef-flavored bouillon

    2 tsp. dried oregano

    1½ tsp. salt

Bring to a boil, reduce heat, and simmer, covered, for 30 minutes.

THE FILLING

While the sauce is simmering, mix together in a large bowl

    1 lb. soft tofu, mashed well with a fork

    1 egg

    ½ cup grated Parmesan cheese

    2 cups grated mozzarella cheese

THE "NOODLES"

Slice in strips about as thick as lasagna noodles

    1 lb. frozen firm tofu, thawed, rinsed, and squeezed dry

Assembling
the Lasagna

Spread about 1/3 of the simmered tomato sauce in the bottom of an oiled 9-inch x 13-inch baking dish.

Place half the tofu slices on the sauce.

Cover with half the filling.

Repeat the layers.

Pour the remaining sauce evenly over the casserole.

Dust with

Grated Parmesan cheese

Bake, covered, at 350° for 45 minutes.

Let stand for 10 minutes before cutting.

stuffed
cabbage leaves

SERVES 4–6

THE LEAVES

1 medium cabbage

Remove the core from the cabbage and steam for 5 minutes over boiling water. Carefully peel off 8–12 outer leaves.

THE FILLING

Sauté in 3 tbs. olive oil

    1 medium onion, chopped

    1 bell pepper, chopped

    4 large cloves garlic, minced

Remove from heat and stir in

    1–1½ lbs. frozen firm tofu, thawed, rinsed, squeezed dry, and crumbled

    1 can (15 oz.) tomato sauce

    3 eggs, lightly beaten

    1 cup cooked rice

    ¼ cup raisins

    ½ tsp. salt

    ½ tsp. paprika

    ¼ tsp. pepper

THE GARNISH

Mix well in a large bowl

    1 medium onion, sliced in rings or half-rings

    1 medium bell pepper, chopped

    4 large cloves garlic, minced

    ¼ cup raisins

THE SAUCE

Mix together in a medium bowl

    1 can (15 oz.) tomato sauce

    ¼ cup water

    ¼ tsp. salt

    ¼ tsp. pepper

ASSEMBLING THE CABBAGE LEAVES

Put ¼ cup of the filling in the center of either 1 large or 2 smaller overlapping leaves.

Fold the ends of the leaf in and roll it around the filling.

Place the rolled leaves close together in an oiled, 5-quart covered casserole.

Spread the garnish evenly over the rolls.

Pour the sauce (mixed with any remaining filling) over the casserole.

Bake, covered, at 350° for 1 hour.

Serve with a large spoon to avoid breaking the rolls.

crepes with tofu and mushrooms

The perpetually pleasing crepe houses tofu in simplicity and elegance —a lovely gift for company.

THE CREPES

Mix in a blender until smooth

> 3 large eggs
> ½ cup milk
> 2 tbs. melted butter
> ¼ tsp. honey
> ½ cup flour
> Dash of salt
> Pepper to taste

Set aside for 1 hour.

Heat a 7-inch crepe pan. Coat the pan lightly with butter. Cover the bottom of the pan with 3 tablespoons of the crepe batter. Swirl and tilt the pan to distribute the batter evenly. When the bottom of the crepe is lightly browned, turn and brown the other side.

Stack the finished crepes on a plate.

THE FILLING

Sauté in 2 tbs. butter or oil

> 2 cups sliced mushrooms
> ½ cup chopped green onion
> 1 clove garlic minced

Remove from the pan. Set aside.

Mix together, in the same pan, over low heat

    2 tbs. butter or oil

    2 tbs. flour

    2 tsp. chicken-flavored bouillon

Add slowly, stirring constantly

    ½ cup milk

Cook, stirring constantly, until thickened.

Remove from heat and stir in

    1 lb. frozen firm tofu, thawed, rinsed,

        squeezed dry, and crumbled

    ½ of the mushroom mixture (but all its liquid)

    ½ cup sour cream

    2 tbs. dry sherry

    ½ tsp. salt

    ¼ tsp. pepper or a few grains cayenne

ASSEMBLING THE CREPES

Spoon 1/8 of the filling down the center of each crepe.

Fold the ends in and roll the crepe around the filling.

Place 2 crepes, seam-side down, on each of 4 broiler-proof plates.

Top with

    ½ cup grated swiss cheese

    The remaining mushrooms

Broil 4 inches from heat until the cheese melts.

Serve immediately.

eggplant and frozen tofu in **casserole**

SERVES 4–6

Sauté in 1–2 tbs. olive oil

    1 onion, chopped

    1 small bell pepper, chopped

Remove from heat and stir in

    1 can (16 oz.) tomatoes, broken up

    1 lb. frozen firm tofu, thawed, rinsed,
       squeezed dry, and crumbled

    ½ tsp. salt

    ¼ tsp. pepper

Spread in the bottom of a 9-inch by 13-inch baking dish

    ¼ of a can (15 oz.) tomato sauce

Top with half the slices from

    1 medium eggplant, cut in ¼-inch rounds

Spread half the tofu mixture on the eggplant rounds.

Cover the tofu mixture with half the slices from

    8–10 oz. mozzarella cheese, thinly sliced

Repeat eggplant, tofu, and cheese layers.

Mix in a medium bowl

    The rest of the tomato sauce

    ½ tsp. dried oregano

    ½ tsp. dried basil

    ¼ cup water

Pour evenly over the casserole.

Top with

       2 tbs. grated Parmesan cheese

Bake, covered, at 375° for 20 minutes.

Remove cover and bake for an additional 20 minutes.

Let stand for 15 minutes before cutting.

tofu breads

tofu pancakes

MAKES ABOUT 18 PANCAKES

Mix in a blender until smooth

    1½ cups milk

    3 eggs

    1 lb. soft tofu

    1 tsp.–1 tbs. oil

    2 tbs. honey

    1 tsp. baking powder

    1 tsp. vanilla

    ¼ tsp. salt

Add and blend again

    1 cup whole-wheat flour

Bake on a lightly oiled, medium-hot griddle until done.

very special
french toast

SERVES 6

Mix in a blender until smooth

> 6–8 eggs
>
> 1½ lbs. soft tofu
>
> ½ tsp. cinnamon
>
> ½ tsp. salt
>
> ¼ cup honey
>
> 2 tsp. vanilla

Place in a single layer in the bottom of an oiled 9-inch x 13-inch pan.

> 6 slices of bread

Pour the tofu mixture evenly over the bread.

Sprinkle with

> ½ tsp. cinnamon

Bake at 350° for 30 minutes or until set.

Serve with maple syrup if desired.

APPLESAUCE VARIATION

Before pouring the tofu mixture over the bread, spoon

> ⅓ cup thick applesauce

on each slice.

pan-fried
corn cakes

MAKES 14–16 CAKES

Mix together in a large bowl

> 1 cup soft tofu, mashed well with a fork
>
> 1 egg, lightly beaten
>
> ⅓ cup melted butter
>
> ¼ cup milk
>
> ¾ cup whole-wheat flour
>
> ¾ tsp. salt
>
> 2 cups whole kernel corn
>
> 2 tbs. chopped green onion
>
> 1½ tsp. baking powder
>
> ¾ tsp. salt
>
> ¼ tsp. pepper

Drop by tablespoons onto a hot, oiled griddle.

Fry to a golden brown on both sides.

tofu chapaties

Mix in a blender until smooth

    1 lb. soft tofu

    ½ cup butter

    1½ tsp. salt

    2 tbs. baking powder

Turn into a large bowl.

Stir in

    3 cups whole-wheat flour

Beat the dough for about 1 minute, until it becomes somewhat smooth and elastic.

Divide the dough into 16 equal parts. Roll each part into an 8-inch round on a floured surface.

Bake each chapati in an ungreased skillet over medium-high heat until done but not brown.

Stack the finished chapaties on a plate.

tofu waffles

Mix in a blender until smooth

    4 eggs

    ¾ cup milk or water

    1 lb. soft tofu

    2 tbs. honey

    ¼ tsp. salt

    1 tsp. baking powder

    1 tsp. vanilla

Add and blend again

    ¾ cup whole-wheat flour

Bake in a preheated waffle iron according to manufacturer's directions.

Stir the batter before pouring each waffle.

eggless waffles

MAKES 4 LARGE WAFFLES

Mix in a blender until smooth
> 1¼ cups milk
> 1 lb. soft tofu
> 2 tbs. honey
> ¼ tsp. salt
> 1 tsp. baking powder
> 1 tsp. vanilla

Add and blend again
> 1 cup whole-wheat flour

Bake in a preheated waffle iron according to manufacturer's directions.

Stir the batter before pouring each waffle.

weight watcher's
waffle

Mix in a blender until smooth

> 1 lb. soft tofu
>
> 4 eggs
>
> 2 tbs. honey
>
> 1 tsp. vanilla
>
> Dash salt
>
> ¼ cup whole-wheat flour

Bake in a preheated waffle iron according to manu-facturer's directions.

Stir the batter before pouring each waffle.

carob
dessert waffles

Mix in a blender until smooth
½ cup milk
½ cup light molasses
¼ cup honey
3 eggs
1 lb. soft tofu
4 tbs. carob powder
3 tbs. oil
¼ tsp. salt
1½ tsp. baking powder
Add and blend again
1 cup whole-wheat flour
Bake in a preheated waffle iron according to manufacturer's directions.
Stir the batter before pouring each waffle.

tofu raisin
bread

Great with apricot preserves!

Mix well in a large bowl

> 2 cups whole-wheat flour
>
> ½ cup raisins

Mix in a blender until smooth

> 2 eggs
>
> 1 lb. soft tofu
>
> ¼ cup honey
>
> ¼ cup butter
>
> 4 tsp. baking powder
>
> ¼ tsp. baking soda
>
> ¼ tsp. salt

Pour the blended ingredients into the flour mixture. Stir well.

Turn into a buttered and floured 8-inch spring form pan.

Bake at 350° for 45 minutes or until a toothpick inserted into the center comes out clean.

Cool 10 minutes in the pan; remove to a rack.

tofu
brown bread

Mix well in a large bowl

>1 cup corn meal
>
>1 cup rye flour
>
>1 cup whole-wheat flour
>
>1 cup raisins

Mix in a blender until smooth

>2 eggs
>
>1 lb. soft tofu
>
>¾ cup light molasses
>
>1 tsp. salt
>
>2 tsp. baking soda
>
>1 tsp. lemon juice

Pour the blended ingredients into the flour mixture.

Beat well with a spoon (or use an electric mixer.)

Turn into 2 buttered 1-quart cans. Fill ¾ full.

Cover the cans with aluminum foil and tie, tape, or rubberband securely in place.

Place the cans on a rack (or a vegetable steamer) in a deep pot. Add enough water to come up 2 inches on the sides of the cans. Cover the pot.

Steam for 3 hours. (The water should continue to boil gently throughout the steaming process. Add more water if it gets low.)

Cool for 10 minutes. Remove from the cans.

Serve hot.

dumplings

Mix in a blender until smooth

    8 oz. soft tofu

    1 egg

    2 tsp. baking powder

    ¼ tsp. salt

Add   2 sprigs fresh parsley, finely chopped

    ½ cup whole-wheat flour

Blend again. Use a spatula to keep the mixture in the blades if necessary.

Drop by teaspoonfuls onto the top of a stew or a thick soup.

Cover tightly and simmer the stew or soup for 15–20 minutes while the dumplings steam.

Don't peek during the first 15 minutes!

yorkshire **pudding**

MAKES 4 GENEROUS SERVINGS

Preheat the oven to 400°.

Mix in a blender until smooth

>3 eggs
>
>1 lb. soft tofu
>
>1 tsp. salt

Add and mix again

>¾ cup unbleached white flour

Melt in a 9-inch x 13-inch baking dish in the preheating oven   ½ cup (1 cube) butter

Pour the tofu mixture slowly into the baking dish.

Do not stir.

Bake for 20 minutes.

Reduce heat to 350° and bake for an additional 10–15 minutes.

Cut into squares and serve immediately.

tofu parmesan
crescents

MAKES 32 ROLLS

Mix in a blender until smooth
> 1 lb. soft tofu
> ¾ cup butter, softened
> ¼ cup Parmesan cheese
> 1 tsp. salt
> 2 tsp. baking powder

Pour into a large bowl.

Using an electric mixer, beat in
> 2 cups whole-wheat flour

Beat the dough for about 1 minute, until it becomes elastic and smooth.

Divide the dough into 4 equal parts. Roll each part into a 10-inch round.

Sprinkle with
> Grated Parmesan cheese

Cut into 8 wedges.

Starting at the wider edge, roll up each wedge.

Place with the center point down, 2 inches apart on an oiled baking sheet.

Tuck the ends in slightly and curve down to form a crescent shape.

Bake at 375° for 30–35 minutes.

sesame
bread sticks

MAKES 32 STICKS

Mix in a blender until smooth

    1 lb. soft tofu

    ¾ cup butter, softened

    1½ tsp. salt

    2½ tsp. baking powder

Pour into a large bowl.

Beat in using an electric mixer,

    ½ cup toasted sesame seeds

    2¼–2½ cups whole-wheat flour

Beat the dough for 1–1½ minutes, until it becomes elastic and smooth.

Divide the dough in 32 parts. Roll each part into a stick about 4–5 inches long.

Place 1 inch apart on an oiled baking sheet. Bake at 375° for 30–35 minutes.

Serve warm or cool.

cornbread
or muffins

Great served piping hot with molasses!

Preheat the oven to 425°.

Mix in a blender until smooth

  1 lb. soft tofu

  2 eggs

  3 tbs. oil

  ¼ cup honey

  1 cup instant nonfat milk powder

  ¼ cup whole-wheat flour

  1 tsp. salt

  1½ tsp. baking powder

  ½ tsp. baking soda

Pour into a large bowl.

Stir in   1½ cups cornmeal

Turn into an oiled 9-inch x 9-inch pan or into 12 oiled muffin tins.

Bake at 425° for 25–30 minutes. (Muffins will take less time.)

cinnamon
oat muffins

Mix well in a large bowl

    1 cup whole-wheat flour

    1 cup rolled oats

    ¼ cup raisins (optional)

Mix in a blender until smooth

    8 oz. soft tofu

    2 eggs

    ¼ cup oil

    ½ cup honey

    1½ tsp. cinnamon

    ½ tsp. salt

    2 tsp. baking powder

    ¼ tsp. baking soda

Pour the blended ingredients into the flour mixture. Stir well.

Fill oiled muffin tins two-thirds full.

Bake at 425° for 12–15 minutes.

crispy crumbles
or **croutons**

Cut into ½ -inch squares

>1 lb. frozen firm tofu, thawed, rinsed, and squeezed dry

Season as desired.

Toast in a broiler or a toaster oven on a lightly oiled baking sheet until dried and crunchy. Turn as needed.

VARIATIONS

TOFU CROUTONS

After the tofu is toasted toss it with

>2–3 tbs. melted butter

Return it to the oven and bake at 350° for an additional 10–15 minutes.

CHEESE TOFU CROUTONS

Sprinkle hot toasted tofu squares with

>1½ tbs. finely grated cheese

breadless **toast**

Slice into bread-shaped pieces about ½-inch wide
1 lb. frozen firm tofu, thawed, rinsed, and
squeezed dry
Toast on each side in a broiler or a toaster oven on a
lightly oiled baking sheet until browned and crunchy.
Once toasted, tofu toast can be reheated in a conventional pop-up toaster.

tofu
desserts

best-ever
rice pudding

Good hot or cold.

Mix in a blender until smooth

1 lb. soft tofu

3 eggs

1 cup honey

2 tsp. lemon juice

½ grated lemon rind

1 tbs. vanilla

½ tsp. salt

½ tsp. cinnamon

Pour into a large bowl.

Stir in   1 cup cooked rice

1 cup unsweetened dried, shredded coconut

¾ cup raisins

Turn into an oiled 2-quart casserole.

Bake at 350° for 1 hour.

lemony
bread pudding

SERVES 4

Mix in a blender until smooth

4 eggs

1 lb. soft tofu

1 cup honey

½ cup water or milk

2 tbs. lemon juice

1 tsp. grated lemon rind

¼ tsp. salt

Add and mix gently with a long-handled spoon

2 cups dried bread cubes (½-inch square)

Pour into a buttered 2-quart casserole.

Sprinkle with

Nutmeg (optional)

Bake at 350° for 35–45 minutes.

tofu mini-pies

Mix in a blender until smooth. Use a spatula to keep the dough in the blades if necessary.

> 1 cup butter
>
> 1 lb. very fresh soft tofu
>
> ¼ tsp. salt

Turn into a large bowl and stir in

> 2–2½ cups whole-wheat flour

Work the mixture until a soft dough is formed. Cover and chill thoroughly.

Using a floured rolling pin, roll the dough out into a rectangle approximately 18 inches x 24 inches.

Cut into 3-inch squares.

In the center of each square drop

> 1 tsp. preserves

Fold the dough over to form a triangle and press the edges together to seal.

Prick and bake on an oiled sheet at 375° for 30 minutes.

tofu cheesecake

Prepare your favorite cheesecake crumb crust in an 8-inch spring form pan or deep dish pie pan.

Mix in a blender until smooth

> 2 eggs
>
> 1 lb. very fresh soft tofu
>
> 1 cup honey
>
> 8 oz. cream cheese, softened
>
> 3 tbs. lemon juice
>
> 1 tbs. grated lemon rind
>
> 1½ tsp. vanilla
>
> Dash of salt

Turn into the prepared crust or a lightly battered 8-inch baking dish.

Bake at 350° for 1 hour.

Chill thoroughly.

tofu custard

Mix in a blender until smooth

> 4 eggs
>
> 1 lb. very fresh soft tofu
>
> 1 cup honey
>
> ½ cup milk
>
> ¼ tsp. salt
>
> 1 tbs. vanilla
>
> 1 tsp. lemon juice

Pour into either custard cups or a 2-quart casserole.

Sprinkle with

> Nutmeg

Place the cups or the casserole in a large pan.

Pour water into the pan until it is halfway up the sides of the custard dish(---).

Bake custard cups at 350° for 25–35 minutes or until set.

Bake the 2-quart casserole at 350° for 45 minutes to 1 hour.

Serve thoroughly chilled.

VARIATIONS:

LEMON CUSTARD

Prepare the **Tofu Custard**. Reduce the vanilla to 1 tsp.
Omit the nutmeg sprinkle.
Add   2 tsp. grated lemon rind
           2 tbs. lemon juice

ALMOND CUSTARD

Prepare the **Tofu Custard**. Reduce the vanilla to 1 tsp.
Omit the lemon juice and the nutmeg sprinkle.
Add   ½ tsp. almond extract

COCONUT CUSTARD

Prepare the **Tofu Custard**. Omit the nutmeg sprinkle.
Add   ½ cup shredded dried unsweetened
           coconut

CUSTARD PIE

Prepare your favorite single 9-inch crust.
Partially bake the crust at 425° for 8 minutes.
Reduce the oven temperature to 350°.
Pour any of the above custards into a partially baked
crust. Continue baking at 350° for 45 minutes, or
until set.

pumpkin
pudding

Mix in a blender until smooth

    2 cups cooked pumpkin (canned or fresh)

    1 lb. very fresh soft tofu

    1 cup honey

    ⅓ cup orange juice

    1 cup instant nonfat milk powder

    4 eggs

    ¼ tsp. salt

    1 tbs. cinnamon

    1 tsp. grated orange rind

    ½ tsp. ground ginger

    ¼ tsp. ground cloves

    2 tsp. vanilla

Pour the blended ingredients into a 9-inch square baking dish.

Bake at 350° for 1 hour or until a knife inserted in the center comes out clean.

Chill thoroughly.

spicy tofu cookies

Mix well in a large bowl

    1½ cups whole-wheat flour

    ½ cup raisins

    ½ cup finely chopped walnuts

    ½ cup chopped dates

    ½ tsp. baking soda

Mix in a blender until smooth

    ½ cup butter, softened

    ⅔ cup honey

    1 egg

    8 oz. soft tofu

    1 tsp. ground ginger

    1 tsp. ground cinnamon

    ½ tsp. ground nutmeg

    ½ tsp. salt

    1 tsp. vanilla

Pour the blended ingredients into the flour mixture.

Stir well.

Drop by teaspoonfuls onto an oiled baking sheet.

Bake at 400° for 10–15 minutes.

steamed
Christmas pudding

Mix well in a large bowl

      1½ cups whole-wheat flour

      3½ tsp. baking powder

Add and mix again

      1 cup chopped dates or figs

      1 cup chopped walnuts

Mix in a blender until smooth

      1 egg

      1 lb. soft tofu

      ½ cup honey

      ½ cup light molasses

      2 tbs. oil

      ½ tsp. vanilla

      ¼ tsp. salt

Pour the blended ingredients into the flour mixture.

Mix well. Turn into a buttered 5-pound honey can. Fill three-quarters full.

Cover the can with aluminum foil and tie, tape, or rubberband securely in place.

Place the can on a rack (or a vegetable steamer) in a deep pot. Add enough boiling water to come halfway up the sides of the can. Cover the pot.

Steam for 2 hours. (The water should continue to boil gently throughout the steaming process. Add more water if it gets low.)

Cool for 10 minutes. Remove from the can. Serve hot or cold.

seraphina's
carrot cake

Mix in a blender until smooth

> 1 egg
>
> ½ cup oil
>
> 1 cup honey
>
> 8 oz. soft tofu
>
> 2 tsp. cinnamon
>
> 2 tsp. baking soda
>
> 2 tsp. vanilla
>
> ½ tsp. salt

Pour into a large bowl.

Using an electric mixer, beat in

> ¾ cup grated carrot
>
> 2 cups whole-wheat flour

Stir in   1 cup chopped walnuts

Turn into two 8-inch oiled and floured cake pans or fill 18 well-oiled muffin tins two-thirds full.

Bake at 325° for 40–45 minutes for cake rounds, 30–35 minutes for cupcakes.

When cool, frost with **Seraphina's Cream Cheese Frosting**, if desired.

**CAROB
CARROT CAKE**

Prepare Seraphina's Carrot Cake.

Omit the cinnamon.

Add   6 tbs. carob powder

Bake as directed above.

**SERAPHINA'S
CREAM CHEESE
FROSTING**

Beat with an electric mixer until creamy and easy to spread   1 cup cream cheese

               2 tbs. honey

               2 tsp. vanilla

simply super
fruit cobbler

Prepare your favorite fruit filling in an 8-inch baking dish.

Bake at 350° until bubbly.

Remove from oven.

COBBLER TOPPING **Mix** together well in a medium-sized bowl

    4 oz. soft tofu

    1 tbs. butter, softened

Add and mix again

    1 egg

    1 tbs. honey

    1 tsp. baking powder

    ¼ tsp. salt

Stir in   ¾ cup whole-wheat flour

Mix until well blended.

Spoon Cobbler Topping in a fairly even layer on top of the fruit.

Bake at 350° for 30 minutes.

Serve warm with cream or vanilla ice cream.

zabaglione

A light, chilled wine custard. A very adult dessert.

Mix in a blender until smooth

> 3 egg yolks
>
> 12 oz. very fresh soft tofu
>
> ⅓ cup honey
>
> ½ cup marsala or dry sherry wine
>
> 1½ tsp. vanilla
>
> ⅛ tsp. salt
>
> ⅛ tsp. nutmeg

Whip in a large bowl until stiff

> 3 egg whites

Gently fold the blended ingredients into the egg whites. Pour into either an 8-inch x 8-inch casserole or custard cups.

Sprinkle with

> Cinnamon

Place the cups or the casserole in a large pan. Pour water into the pan until it is halfway up the sides of the custard dish(es).

Bake at 350° for 30–35 minutes or until a knife inserted in the center comes out clean.

Serve thoroughly chilled.

Garnish with

> Slivered toasted almonds

mellow
pudding

Mix in a blender until smooth

    2 eggs

    1 lb. very fresh soft tofu

    ½ cup butter

    1 cup light molasses

    1 cup honey

    ½ tsp. baking soda

Add and blend again

    ½ cup whole-wheat flour

Turn into an oiled 2-quart casserole.

Bake at 350° for 45 minutes or until firm.

Serve with whipped cream.

FRUIT VARIATION

Stir in before baking

    1 cup finely chopped walnuts

    1 cup raisins or chopped pitted dates

Bake and serve as directed.

carob pudding *or* pie filling

Soften in ½ cup water

>   2 tbs. unflavored gelatin

Heat to dissolve thoroughly.

Mix in a blender until smooth

>   1 lb. very fresh soft tofu
>
>   1 cup light molasses or ¾ cup light molasses
>   and 2 tbs. honey
>
>   ½ cup water
>
>   3 tbs. carob powder
>
>   ¼ tsp. salt
>
>   ½ tsp. vanilla
>
>   The gelatin mixture

Whip in a large bowl until stiff

>   ½ pint whipping cream

Gently fold the blended ingredients into the whipped cream. Turn into a pudding mold or 2 baked 9-inch pie shells.

Chill overnight.

apple-spice
delight

Great with butter and maple syrup.

Soak in ½ cup milk

2 slices dried bread, broken up

Mix well in a medium-sized bowl

4 eggs, lightly beaten

8 oz. very fresh soft tofu, mashed well with a
fork or potato masher

1 large apple, grated

2 tbs. honey

½ tsp. cinnamon

½ tsp. vanilla

¼ tsp. salt

Stir in the soaked bread.

Turn into a buttered 8-inch round baking pan.

Bake at 375° for 20-25 minutes or until set.

favorite
crumb crust

This is a very easy, delicious way to make use of a dry bread. Use the smaller amounts for an 8-inch pan, the larger for a 10-inch one.

Mix well in a medium bowl

      1–1½ cups very fine dried bread crumbs

      4–6 tbs. dark brown sugar

      4–6 tbs. melted butter

      1 tsp. cinnamon

Pat into an 8-inch or 10-inch spring form pan or pie pan.

Bake, if desired, at 325° for 15 minutes. Otherwise, chill until needed.

applesauce
torte

THE CRUST (OPTIONAL)

Prepare the preceding Crumb Crust for a 10-inch spring form pan.

Reserve ¼ cup of the crumb mixture.

Put the remaining mixture into a 10-inch spring form pan.

THE FILLING

Mix in a blender until smooth

    3 eggs

    1 lb. very fresh soft tofu

    1 cup honey

    ¼ cup whole-wheat flour

    2 tbs. lemon juice

    2 tbs. grated lemon rind

    1 tsp. ground cinnamon

    ¼ tsp. nutmeg

    1 tsp. vanilla

Turn into a large mixing bowl.

Stir in   2 cups unsweetened applesauce

Pour into the crust.

Top with the reserved crumbs.

Bake at 350° for 1 hour.

Chill overnight.

egg nog torte

**THE CRUST
(OPTIONAL)**

Prepare your favorite crumb crust for an 8-inch spring form pan.

THE FILLING

Mix in a blender until smooth

      1½ cups egg nog

      8 oz. very fresh soft tofu

      2 eggs

      ⅓ cup honey

      2 tbs. brandy

Turn into the prepared crust or a buttered 8-inch baking dish.

Bake at 325° for 1 hour.

Chill thoroughly.

peachy pie
phenomenon

Prepare your favorite single 9-inch crust. (optional)

Mix in a medium-sized bowl

> 2½ cups thinly sliced peaches
>
> ½ cup unsweetened dried, shredded coconut
>
> ¼ cup honey
>
> 2 tbs. whole-wheat flour
>
> ½ tsp. ground cinnamon
>
> ⅛ tsp. ground nutmeg

Turn into the crust or a buttered 9-inch baking dish.

Dot with 1 tbs. butter (optional)

Mix in a blender until smooth

> 2 eggs
>
> 12 oz. very fresh soft tofu
>
> 4 oz. cream cheese, softened
>
> ¾ cup honey
>
> ½ tsp. ground cinnamon
>
> ¼ tsp. salt
>
> 1½ tsp. vanilla

Gently pour the blended ingredients over the peaches. Do not stir.

Bake at 350° for 50–60 minutes.

Serve warm or chilled.

carrot pie

THE CRUST

(OPTIONAL)

Prepare your favorite single 9-inch crust.

Bake at 400° for 5 minutes.

THE FILLING

Mix in a blender until smooth

2 cups chopped cooked carrots

¾ cup honey

¼ cup light molasses

1 egg

1 tsp. vanilla

½ tsp. salt

½ tsp. ground ginger

½ tsp. ground cinnamon

¼ tsp. ground nutmeg

¼ tsp. allspice

Add and blend again

12 oz. very fresh soft tofu

Add and mix gently with a long-handled spoon

¼ cup raisins (optional)

Turn into the pie shell or a lightly oiled 9-inch baking dish.

Bake at 350° for 50–60 minutes or until a knife inserted in the center comes out clean.

Chill thoroughly.

perfection
plum prize

Substitute golden delicious apples, when plums are out of season.

THE CRUST

Mix well in a medium-sized bowl
    1½ cups unbleached flour
    ¼ cup brown sugar
    ¼ tsp. salt
Cut in with a pastry blender or two knives
    ½ cup butter, softened
Work with hands to form a ball.
Press the dough into the bottom of a buttered
9-inch x 9-inch x 2-inch baking pan.

FRUIT FILLING

Mix well in a medium-sized bowl
    4 cups thinly sliced Italian prune plums
    2 tbs. flour
    ½ cup honey
    1½ tsp. cinnamon
Spread over the prepared crust.

THE CUSTARD **Mix** in a blender until smooth

2 eggs

½ cup honey

12 oz. very fresh soft tofu

½ cup (4 oz.) cream cheese

1½ tsp. vanilla

½ tsp. cinnamon

½ tsp. grated lemon rind

Gently pour the blended ingredients over the fruit. Do not stir.

Bake at 350° for 1 hour.

Chill thoroughly before serving.

yam pie

THE CRUST
(OPTIONAL)

Prepare your favorite single 9-inch crust.
Bake at 400° for 8 minutes.

THE FILLING

Mix in a blender until smooth

2 cups puréed cooked yams
1 lb. very fresh soft tofu
1 cup orange juice
½ cup butter
½ cup honey
¼ cup light molasses
2 eggs
1½ tsp. grated lemon rind
½ tsp. salt
¼ tsp. ground nutmeg
1 tsp. vanilla

Turn into the pie shell or a lightly oiled 9-inch baking dish.

Bake at 350° for 35–40 minutes or until set.

Chill thoroughly.

Index

BOOKS BY THE CROSSING PRESS

Bill Taylor Cooks Chicken
By Bill Taylor

As former Corporate Chef at The Crossing Press, Bill Taylor has prepared hundreds of chicken dishes and has chosen the very best for this book. "I watch the fat content of every dish I prepare and find that people don't really miss the fat as long as the food is tasty. On this score, I get feedback after every meal and the votes are clearly in—people here really like the way I cook."

$12.95 • Paper • ISBN 1-58091-045-9

Good Food: The Comprehensive Food and Nutrition Resource

By Margaret M. Wittenberg

An exceptionally well-organized, up-to-date, and easily accessible treatise on food and nutrition. Wittenberg delineates a direct connection between food and quality of life.
—Susan Jane Cheney, Food Writer/Columnist

$18.95 • Paper • ISBN 0-89594-746-3

Innovative Soy Cooking
By Trudie Burnham

This collection of recipes is perhaps the most original kitchen work that has crossed our editor's desk in a long time. Here are tofu, tempeh, and miso dishes we drooled over!

$6.95 • Paper • ISBN 0-89594-962-8

Japanese Vegetarian Cooking

By Patricia Richfield

Easy-to-follow directions, information on techniques, plus a glossary of Japanese ingredients make this a must-have cookbook for all Japanese food fans.

$14.95 • Paper • ISBN 0-89594-805-2

BOOKS BY THE CROSSING PRESS

Noodle Fusion: Asian Pasta Dishes for Western Palates

By Dorothy Rankin

This book has it all: from spring rolls to egg rolls, wontons to pot stickers; from cool salads to comforting soups; from vegetarian delights to deep sea wonders; from chicken and duck, to beef and pork exotica. Included is a clear description of the various Asian noodles, both fresh and dried, which are available in their astonishing array at most supermarkets.

$16.95 • Paper • ISBN 0-89594-956-3

Pestos!: Cooking with Herb Pastes

By Dorothy Rankin

An inventive and tasteful collection-it makes the possibilities of herb pastes enticing.—Publishers Weekly

$8.95 • Paper • ISBN 0-89594-180-5

Salad Dressings

By Teresa H. Burns

This little book is full of creative dressings that are fresh, healthy and delicious.

$6.95 • Paper • ISBN 0-89594-895-8

Sauces for Pasta!

By K. Trabant with A. Chesman

This little book has my favorite new and old sauces.—Grace Kirschenbaum, *World of Cookbooks*

$8.95 • Paper • ISBN 0-89594-403-0

To receive a current catalog from The Crossing Press
please call toll-free, 800-777-1048.
Visit our Web site: **www.crossingpress.com**